Paris Travel Guide for Teens

The easy French guide to discover culture,hidden gems and food to plan an unforgettable trip

TABLE OF CONTENTS

MAP

Scan for more map

Chapter 1

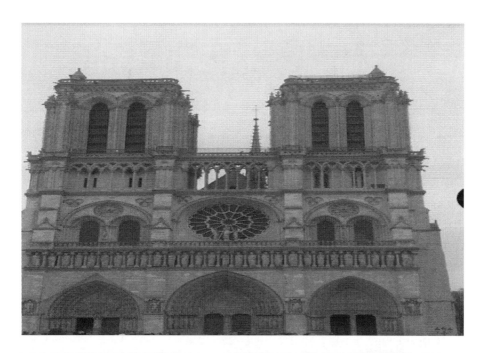

Introduction

Greetings from the enchanted city of Paris, where legends of romance, creativity, and enduring beauty seem to thump beneath each cobblestone. Take a trip beyond travel guides with "Paris Travel Guide For Teens," a voyage created just for the colorful spirits of youth. Imagine exploring Montmartre's hidden treasures and strolling down the Champs-Élysées with the Eiffel Tower by your side, just like a real Parisian would. This book is a passport to seeing the city's pulse through the eyes of teenagers, not just sights. This book is your key to unlocking the youthful magic of Paris, combining adventure, culture, and the exhilaration of exploration, whether you're enthralled by the masterpieces of the Louvre or wanting the newest trends on Rue du Faubourg Saint-Honoré. Experience the City of Lights as your own private playground with this special travel companion designed for adventurous people eager to create lifelong experiences. An incredible journey through a teen's Parisian adventures awaits them in Paris.

Take a thrilling trip through Paris's charming streets with the help of "Paris Travel Guide For Teens." Imagine this: The echoes of ancient stories fill the air as you stroll through the old Marais area, exposing secrets of knights and secret courtyards. Explore the mysteries of the underground catacombs, where bones and skulls tell a terrifying story of bygone eras.

The thrill doesn't end there, though; picture a scene from a movie at the top of Montparnasse Tower, when the city's magnificent view is revealed beneath a starry sky. Take in the lively Latin Quarter's pulse, where each cobblestone appears to be dancing to the sounds of street performers and the laughter of recently made friends.

Discover the tales engraved in Belleville's graffiti-lined alleys as you turn through these pages, along with the famous sites like the Louvre and Notre-Dame. Prepare to embrace the vibrancy of Parisian life, from the thrill of riding the Seine beneath the stars to the stylish stores of Le Marais.

This guide isn't simply about landmarks; it's also a narrative journey, a colorful tapestry woven with the strands of Parisian history, culture, and the endless excitement that awaits any adolescent who is eager to call Paris home. Allow the City of Lights to guide you on an amazing journey through the heart of Paris that is full of tales to tell. This is where your adventure starts.

Brief History of Paris

Known as the "City of Lights," Paris has a rich and interesting past that has influenced its cultural importance. Paris began as a Celtic village known as "Lutetia" about 250 BCE, and in the first century it rose to prominence as a major Roman metropolis. It has seen kingdoms come and fall, seen changes in architecture, and been at the center of both political and artistic movements over the ages.

Famous structures like Notre-Dame Cathedral were built during the medieval era, and the Renaissance era fostered the city's cultural growth. During the Age of Enlightenment, Paris developed into a global cultural hub that promoted advances in philosophy and thought.

The storming of the Bastille served as a symbol of the profound social and political upheavals brought about by the French Revolution in 1789. Napoleon III oversaw urban planning projects in the 19th century that resulted in the construction of famous buildings like the Eiffel Tower and broad boulevards.

Despite suffering during both World Wars I and II, Paris's position as a center of world culture was confirmed by post-war reconstruction and economic growth. Travelers seeking a blend of history, art, and dynamic urban life will find the city to be a timeless destination as it continues to evolve, fusing historical charm with modern innovation.

Why Paris is a great destination for teen

Paris is a fantastic travel destination for teenagers because it provides a distinctive fusion of modern experiences, history, and culture. Teenagers should visit Paris for the following reasons:

Iconic Landmarks: Teens can explore famous sites like the Louvre Museum, Notre Dame Cathedral, and the Eiffel Tower, which will leave them with amazing memories.

Art & Culture: Paris is a global hub for art and culture, giving teenagers access to world-class museums, street art, and exciting live performances.

Fashion Hub: Paris is a fashionista's dream destination for youths. The city, which is well-known for its haute couture, has chic boutiques, antique shops, and opportunities to see the newest styles in clothing.

Gastronomic Adventure: The flavors of French food are a feast for the senses. Teens can savor a wide range of cuisines that go beyond the standard tourist fare, as well as delectable pastries and street food.

Nightlife and Entertainment: From outdoor movie nights to concerts, Paris has teen-friendly entertainment alternatives. At night, the city comes to life and creates a vibrant, pleasant environment.

Chic Lifestyle: By immersing themselves in the elegant and sophisticated Parisian way of life, teenagers can develop a sophisticated and global sense of flair.

Language Learning: Since French is a common language and people in Paris value efforts made in speaking it, visiting Paris is a great way for teenagers to practice and improve their language skills.

Experiences Varying: Paris has something for everyone, from history fans strolling through ancient neighborhoods to tech aficionados interacting with the city's latest developments.

Public Transportation Adventure: Teens can get a sense of freedom by exploring the well-organized and vast Paris public transportation system, which can be an adventure in and of itself.

Youthful Vibe: With its parks, street performances, and a wide range of activities that cater to youngsters' interests and energy levels, Paris radiates a youthful and vibrant vibe.

In conclusion, youth can enjoy a diverse range of experiences in Paris, including the excitement of a bustling urban setting, artistic exploration, and cultural enrichment.

Chapter 2

Getting Ready

Visa and entry requirements

It is essential for visitors to Paris to be aware of the entry and visa procedures. This is a broad summary:

Schengen Area: Paris is included in the Schengen Area, thus if your nation has a visa-waiver agreement or is a member as well, you can enter Paris for brief visits (often up to 90 days in a 180-day period) without a visa.

Requirements for a Visa:

You will probably need to apply for a Schengen Visa if your nation is not included in the Schengen Area or does not have a visa-waiver agreement. Consult the French consulate or embassy in your nation of residence for information on the application procedure and special requirements.

Application Process: Obtain a visa as soon as possible after the trip you want to take. A completed application form, passport-sized pictures, confirmation of travel plans, hotel reservations, travel insurance, and evidence of sufficient funds to cover your stay are typically required papers.

Validity of Passport: Verify that your passport is valid for at least three months after the day you plan to leave the Schengen Area.

Children Traveling Alone: Extra paperwork, such as parental approval and details about the accompanying adult, could be needed if an adolescent is going anywhere by themselves or without the presence of one or both parents.

Health Insurance: Having travel health insurance that covers medical costs and repatriation for the length of your trip is advised.

Rules Regarding Customs:

Learn the rules governing customs as there can be limitations on what you can and cannot bring into the nation.

Airport Procedures: Comply with all airport protocols upon arrival, including passport control and any further inspections. Bring your return ticket, travel documentation, and evidence of lodging with you.

For the most recent and detailed information about entry and visa requirements depending on your nationality, always check the official websites of the French government or embassy. Following these guidelines guarantees a hassle-free and delightful trip to Paris.

Packing tips for teens

Effective packing is essential for a trouble-free and delightful trip to Paris. The following packing advice is intended especially for teenagers:

comfy Shoes: Since there will be a lot of walking in Paris, bring comfy yet fashionable footwear. For exploring the city, sneakers or cozy sandals are excellent choices.

Weather-appropriate Clothes: Make sure your luggage is prepared for the conditions on the days you will be traveling. It's a good idea to layer, and even on summer days, a lightweight jacket or sweater might be handy.

Chic Outfits: Since Parisians are noted for their sense of style, pack a variety of casual and somewhat dressier looks for various settings. Remember to include some stylish accessories!

Chargers and adapters: Be sure to bring chargers for any electrical equipment you may have, such as your phone, camera, or other gadgets.

Reusable Water Bottle: Drink plenty of water as you explore. Refilling a reusable water bottle during the day can save costs and cut down on plastic waste.

Backpack or Day Bag: Bring a compact backpack or day bag to hold necessities such as water, snacks, a map, and any additional goods you may find while out and about.

Travel-Sized Toiletries: In order to conserve space, pack travel-sized toiletries. Add necessities like shampoo, toothpaste, toothbrushes, and any other personal care products you require.

Travel Journal or Blog: Use a travel journal or blog to write about your experiences. It's a fantastic method to document moments and tell loved ones about your travels.

Carry your gadgets with you at all times by using a portable charger. This is especially helpful for extended sightseeing days.

Small Umbrella: The weather in Paris is not always predictable. Have a tiny, collapsible umbrella with you in case of sudden downpours.

Snacks: Keep some non-perishable snacks on hand for on-the-go munching. This is useful for taking lengthy walks or standing in line.

Language Reference or App:

Review fundamental French words and phrases using a language guide or app. This is useful when interacting with people from the area.

Travel-related Games or Reading:

Pack a light game or a nice book for when you have some downtime, whether it's on the way there or just to unwind.

Reusable Shopping Bag: Whether it's for groceries or souvenirs, a foldable, reusable shopping bag comes in handy.

Vital Records:

A separate pouch should be used to hold copies of your passport, travel insurance, and any other critical documents. Giving these copies to a relative or friend back home is also a smart option. You may ensure that you have everything you need for a wonderful trip to Paris by planning ahead and bringing only essential items.

Health and safety considerations

Traveling to any destination, especially Paris, requires taking precautions for your health and safety. For teenagers traveling to the city, keep the following points in mind:

Obtain comprehensive travel insurance that covers unanticipated situations, medical crises, and trip cancellations.

Health Concerns: Before visiting Paris, find out if you need to get any immunizations. Make sure your regular immunizations are current.

Medication: If you require any prescription drugs, make sure you have a sufficient supply with you. In case of an emergency, have a list of your prescriptions with the generic names on it.

Emergency Contacts: Maintain a list of contacts for emergencies, including contacts back home and local emergency numbers. Give your traveling partners this information.

Maintain Hydration:

Especially in the summer and on long hikes, make sure you stay hydrated. Bring a reusable water bottle with you because dehydration can be a problem.

Sun Protection: Especially in the summer, wear sunscreen to protect yourself from the sun. For further protection, think about donning a hat and sunglasses.

Street Safety: Use street smarts and pay attention to your surroundings. Steer clear of dimly lit areas at night and use caution when handling valuables in busy situations.

Public Transportation Safety: Be mindful of the rules regarding safety when using public transportation. Keep an eye out for pickpockets and hold onto your stuff, especially when using public transportation and in crowded areas.

Food Safety: Savor the delectable cuisine, but exercise caution when it comes to cleanliness. Select trustworthy restaurants, and let the staff know if you have any dietary restrictions.

COVID-19 Safety Measures:

Keep yourself updated on any recommendations or restrictions pertaining to COVID-19. As necessary, abide by the safety precautions advised, such as using a mask and avoiding social situations.

Emergency Services: Learn where the closest pharmacy, hospital, and embassy are located. Keep your phone saved with the 112 emergency number for your area.

Legal Aspects to Take into Account:

Respect the rules and laws in your area. Recognize cultural customs to provide a courteous and secure encounter.

Consular Support:

Once there, register with the embassy or consulate of your country. This can be useful in the event of an emergency or the issuance of significant travel advisories.

Remain Up to Date:

Watch for updates on the local weather and news. Keep yourself updated on any circumstances or occurrences that can impact your trip arrangements.

While touring Paris, you can help ensure a safe and pleasurable trip by being alert and adopting the appropriate safety precautions.

Chapter 3

Navigating Paris

Public transportation guide

Using Paris's public transit system is a productive method to get to know the city. This is a how-to guide for teenagers using public transportation:

Metro System: The extensive and well-connected Paris Métro is a subway network. Get acquainted with the metro map, which is made up of numerous lines, each with a unique color and number.

Passes & Tickets:

Purchase travel passes or tickets from vending machines or metro stations. Single tickets, day passes, and longer-term passes are available. You might need your ticket for sporadic checks, so keep it close at hand.

Finding Your Way Around Stations:

Observe the announcements and signage at the station. Stations are clearly identified, and signs are color-coded. To find the right line and direction, refer to the instructions.

Bus System: The areas not covered by the metro are part of Paris's vast bus network. Routes are indicated, and bus stations are properly signposted. The same metro tickets are accepted on buses.

Trains: RER (Réseau Express Régional) trains are an option to consider for routes outside of the city center. They link Paris to big attractions like Disneyland Paris as well as outlying locations.

Transfers: A few metro stations provide service on several lines, making transfers simple. Observe signs designating intersections and consult the metro map to determine the most expedient routes.

Peak Hours: If at all possible, steer clear of public transit during these times. Rush hours in the morning and evening can be congested. Make appropriate travel plans.

Accessibility: Elevators and ramps are common features in metro stations. If necessary, look for stations that have these features.

Safety Advice: Pay attention to your possessions, particularly in busy places. Make sure your bags are safe, watch out for pickpockets, and stay in well-lit places if you are traveling at night.

Options for Biking: There are programs for bike sharing and an expanding network of bike lanes throughout Paris. For an interesting take on the city, think about touring it from two wheels.

Boats on the Seine: Utilize the boats on the Seine River for an attractive voyage. There are passes for public transportation that may include boat rides.

Handy applications: Download applications for public transit to view routes, schedules, and get real-time updates. Two well-known apps are Citymapper and RATP.

Cultural Courtesies:

When taking public transit, abide by certain manners. Assist those in need with seating, and make as little noise as possible.

Language Tip: Acquire a few simple words in French while using public transit. It might be useful when enquiring about or requesting support.

Teens who become proficient with the city's public transit system can quickly tour Paris, learn about its unique districts, and visit its well-known sights.

Currency and money tips

It's crucial to know the exchange rate and practice prudent money management when visiting Paris. The following money and currency advice is for teenagers:

The euro (€):

The Euro (€) is the recognized form of payment in Paris. Learn about the different euro coins and denominations, which range from 1 cent to 2 euros.

Currency exchange: To get better rates, exchange your money at banks or exchange bureaus. Avoid exchanging money at airports because the exchange rates might not be as good.

ATMs: Take out cash in euros via ATMs. To avoid any problems, make sure your card can be used for overseas withdrawals and let your bank know when you will be traveling.

Credit and Debit Cards: In Paris, most major credit and debit cards are accepted. To prevent any problems with card transactions, let your bank know about your trip schedule.

Payments via Contactless Technology:

In Paris, contactless payment methods such as credit/debit cards and smartphone payments are widely used. For convenience, many places accept these methods.

Budgeting: To control your expenditures, establish a daily budget. This involves setting aside money for lodging, entertainment, and food.

Little Denominations: Save your little denominations for modest purchases and daily costs. It's useful for things like metro tickets, food, and gratuities.

Tipping Culture: Most restaurant invoices include a gratuity. Rounding up or adding a little gratuity, though, is appreciated. In cafés and informal dining establishments, tipping is less customary.

Safety precautions:

To avoid theft, use caution when handling your possessions, particularly your wallet and credit cards. Think about carrying a safe travel wallet or a money belt.

Cash for emergencies:

A small sum of cash for emergencies should be kept somewhere else. In the event that your cards are misplaced or rejected, this can be helpful.

Check Exchange Rates: To keep track of the value of your native currency in relation to the euro, check exchange rates on a regular basis. This aids in your ability to make wise financial judgments.

Smart Shopping: Check pricing before committing to a purchase, particularly in popular destinations. Prices at some souvenir shops might be more.

Tax-Free Shopping: Find out if you may shop without paying taxes if you want to make large purchases. Value Added Tax (VAT) refunds are frequently available to non-EU residents.

Terminology for Business Transactions:

Learn some fundamental transactional French, such as how to ask for the bill or get the price of an item confirmed.

Adopting prudent money management habits and remaining educated can allow kids to enjoy their time in Paris without worrying about money.

Basic French phrases for teens

Here are some basic French phrases that teens might find handy during their visit to Paris:

1. Hello/Hi: Bonjour/Salut
2. Goodbye: Au revoir
3. Please: S'il vous plaît (formal)/S'il te plaît (informal)
4. Thank you: Merci
5. You're welcome: De rien
6. Excuse me/Pardon: Excusez-moi (formal)/Pardon (informal)
7. Yes: Oui
8. No: Non
9. I don't understand: Je ne comprends pas
10. Can you help me?: Pouvez-vous m'aider? (formal)/Peux-tu m'aider? (informal)
11. Where is...?: Où est...?
12. How much is this?: Combien ça coûte?

13. I would like...: Je voudrais...

14. What time is it?: Quelle heure est-il?

15. May I have the bill, please?: L'addition, s'il vous plaît

16. Do you speak English?: Parlez-vous anglais?

17. I'm lost: Je suis perdu(e)

18. Can I use the restroom?: Puis-je utiliser les toilettes?

19. My name is...: Je m'appelle...

20. How do I get to...?: Comment puis-je aller à...?

Chapter 4

Must-Visit Attractions

Eiffel Tower

One of the most recognizable structures in the world, the Eiffel Tower is a beloved staple of Paris, the City of Lights. You can take advantage of guided tours to the second- and third-story viewing platforms with these entrance tickets.

Meet your guide at least 15 minutes before the time on your ticket, around five minutes away from the Eiffel Tower. After that, take a quick and stress-free elevator ride up the tower while walking with your group and your guide.

Your guide will be available to provide you with a brief overview of the tower and the city's monuments situated beneath it. View iconic Parisian locations like the Louvre and Basilique du Sacré-Coeur from above.

Proceed through the normal entry to the top, where you may also have a fascinating behind-the-scenes look at the life of the 19th-century French engineer by exploring Gustave Eiffel's private rooms, or purchase a glass of Champagne from the bar.

Ages 4-99, maximum 20 people per group; 1 hour 30 minutes
Start time: Verify the schedule
Mobile pass
English live guide

Louvre Museum

With this skip-the-line tour, you can avoid the long lines at the Louvre Museum, one of Paris's most visited sights, and save a ton of time. Enjoy a guided tour of many of the collection's treasures, including both well-known and obscure pieces, once you're inside. Through art, discover more about the history and cultures of France and Europe. This comprehensive tour is especially enjoyable for art fans.

0–99 years old
Time spent: two hours and thirty minutes
Beginning time: Verify the availability
Mobile ticket Instant manual: Italian, French, Spanish, German, Russian, and English

Priority entry to the Louvre allows you to save time for other sightseeing excursions.
Enjoy individualized attention during a private tour.
A hassle-free method to see a must-see landmark in Paris
Gain more knowledge than you would on a solo museum trip.

The beginning of your journey is directly outside the Louvre Museum's glass pyramids. Get to know your guide and get ready to enter. With special fast-track entry, you can breeze through the lines at the door. Pre-arranged tickets for skip-the-line admittance are included with tours, so you may avoid the lengthy lineup.

Discover the museum's well-known galleries while hearing your private guide narrate stories about the artwork on display (small-group alternatives are also available). You will examine well-known works of art that visitors might otherwise overlook, as well as lesser-known treasures like the mysterious Mona Lisa and the iconic Venus de Milo sculpture.

After the tour is over, you are free to explore the museum on your own thanks to your tickets.

With this interactive half-day experience, you may tour an organic farm and learn how to prepare regional specialties from scratch in addition to enjoying the delicious food that Thailand has to offer. Take part in a cooking class where you can make a range of foods, including curry paste, curry, stir-fry, soup, and spring rolls. You can also get professional tips on how to produce herbs and vegetables.

Notre-Dame Cathedral

Known as "Our Lady of Paris," the famous Notre Dame Cathedral in Paris is a magnificent example of French Gothic design. The significant monument was constructed in the twelfth century and has seen several historical occurrences. Victor Hugo's tale of the Hunchback of

Notre-Dame was also influenced by it. You can view the cathedral's impressive exterior from outside, which is framed by two graceful bell towers, stained glass windows, and a lavishly sculptured front.

For a nominal admission charge, you can also access the cathedral to see Nio-Gothic furnishings and artwork and take part in their monthly meetings.

Ile de la Cité/Ile Saint-Louis is the neighborhood.
In the center of Paris, between the Seine, are two islands. Ile de la Cité, the more spectacular one, is a historical gem. This is the location of the Gothic Sainte-Chapelle, the birthplace of Paris, and the jail where Marie Antoinette was detained prior to her execution. Travelers swarm to view the famous Notre Dame and the exquisite bridges that cross the Seine. The more laid-back island of Ile Saint-Louis greets you with little boutiques, quaint traditional restaurants, and supposedly the best ice cream in the city. From its inception to its contemporary allure, this is Paris at its core.

Contact information

+33 1 42 34 56 10

Montmartre and Sacré-Cœur

The Mercure Paris Montmartre Sacré Coeur hotel is situated at the base of Sacré Coeur, near to the Haussmann-Opéra district's shops and the Moulin Rouge. Its rooms are modern and roomy. The hotel is conveniently located near major tourist attractions like the Eiffel Tower, Champs Elysées, La Défense business district, Carrefour Pleyel, and the Stade de France, making it an ideal choice for both business and romantic weekends in Paris.

Property features

Nearby, there is pay public parking.

Free WiFi and high-speed internet

Bar / lounge

Patio

Dogs and other friendly pets are welcome.

cab service

Internet-connected business center

banquet space

Features of the room

Dark-colored drapes

rooms that are soundproof

Air conditioning

Cleaning Services

Room service

Tea/coffee maker

TV via cable or satellite

Shower or bathtub

Seine River Cruise

In search of a romantic Parisian dinner cruise?
You may enjoy excellent food and entertainment at The Diamant Bleu.

Join us for a Seine River Cruise on this panoramic yacht and visit the famous Parisian landmarks while savoring our chef's three-course meal.
During our two hours and thirty minute trip, let Paris reveal itself to you starting at the National Library and continuing past the Statue of Liberty, Notre Dame Cathedral, Conciergerie, Concorde Square, and major historical bridges.
Enjoy our expansive patio at your leisure; it's open to you the entire journey. Enjoying a cup of champagne or one of our chef's delectable cocktails while taking a selfie with the Eiffel Tower is the ideal activity.

View our example menu here.
There is no menu for children available.
Seasons affect the content.

Chapter 5

Adventurous Experiences

Disneyland Paris

In the center of Europe, Disneyland Paris is a magnificent place that provides a distinctive Disney experience. Here is a quick rundown of Disneyland Paris for teenagers, along with some advice:

Location: About 32 kilometers east of Paris, near Marne-la-Vallée, is where you can find Disneyland Paris. You can get there quickly by vehicle and train.

Parks: Disneyland Park and Walt Disney Studios Park are the two theme parks that make up Disneyland Paris. Every park has a unique lineup of entertainment, shows, and attractions.

Attractions: Take pleasure in a variety of exhilarating rides, vintage Disney attractions, and exclusive experiences. There is something to suit the tastes of every teen, from well-known attractions like Space Mountain to the captivating Sleeping Beauty Castle.

Entertainment: Don't miss the character meet-and-greets, live shows, and parades. Make plans for the day so you can see your favorite Disney characters in action by checking the performance schedule.

FastPass: Use the FastPass system to get around the typical lineups at well-liked attractions. This lets you make the most of your time and go on more rides.

Download the official Disneyland Paris app on your smartphone. It offers up-to-date details on ride wait times, show times, and interactive park maps to make your navigation easier.

Dining possibilities: Take advantage of the many possibilities for dining in the parks, ranging from themed restaurants to quick service restaurants. For popular restaurants, consider booking reservations in advance.

Souvenirs: Browse the several stores located throughout the parks to purchase Disney apparel and mementos. It's a wonderful method to save memories of your enchanted encounter at home.

Disney characters may come to your table during your lunch if you choose to reserve a character dining experience. Engaging with your beloved characters can be an enjoyable experience. Disney PhotoPass: Purchase this service to obtain high-quality images of your unforgettable experiences. This lets you enjoy the parks more while leaving the photos to the experts.

Events & Themed Seasons: Look through the calendar for special occasions like Halloween and Christmas celebrations, as well as themed seasons. These happenings give your visit an additional dimension of charm.

Transportation: To get to Disneyland Paris if you're staying in central Paris, think about taking the quick and easy RER train system. The trip takes roughly forty minutes.

To ensure a fantastic experience, make sure to schedule your visit well in advance, rank your top attractions, and fully immerse yourself in the magical world of Disneyland Paris.

Catacombs of Paris

More than six million people's remains are kept in the Catacombs of Paris, an underground ossuary located in the center of the city. Teens who would like to explore this distinctive and historic site can find the following information useful:

Where:

The official entrance to the Catacombs is located at 1 Avenue du Colonel Henri Rol-Tanguy. The Catacombs are located beneath the streets of Paris.
Past:

In the late 18th century, the overcrowding in Paris's cemeteries gave rise to the idea of the Catacombs. The bones were moved to the deserted quarries under the city from different cemeteries.
Admission and Guided Tour:

After descending a spiral staircase into the underground tunnels, visitors arrive through a modest entrance. A section of the extensive network of tunnels is explored throughout the tour, which features thoughtfully organized skulls and bones.
Bone Configurations:

The Catacombs have a horrific yet fascinating atmosphere because to the creative arrangements of bones, such as walls constructed of piled skulls and femurs.
Tours with a guide:

There are guided excursions that offer anecdotes and historical background about the Catacombs. Joining a tour is advised for a more rewarding experience.
Conditions and Temperature:

It is always cool in the Catacombs, so pack a light sweater or jacket. Wear comfortable shoes because the routes can be bumpy and small.
Snapshots:

Although you are welcome to take pictures, please respect the site's serious atmosphere. In general, flash photography is not allowed.
Tickets and Schedule:

Get your tickets in advance to beat the crowds. The Catacombs are open most days of the week; however, for the most recent information on hours, visit the official website.
Taking Age Into Account:

Because of the nature of the place, the Catacombs might not be appropriate for extremely young children or others who might find the experience unpleasant.
Nearby Points of Interest:

To give further historical context, schedule your visit to neighboring sights like the Paris Catacombs Museum and the Montparnasse Cemetery.
Behaving with Respect:

As with any historical site, show consideration for others and abide by any instructions given by staff. It is a location with a distinct past that calls for consideration.
For those who are interested in learning more about Paris's hidden mysteries, a visit to the Catacombs of Paris provides an intriguing look into the city's past as well as a singular and unforgettable experience.

Parc des Buttes-Chaumont

Paris's 19th arrondissement is home to the lovely public park known as Parc des Buttes-Chaumont. Teens who would like to explore this verdant haven can find the following information:

Location: The park is conveniently close to public transit and is located in Paris' northeastern region. 1 Rue Botzaris, 75019 Paris, France is the address.

History: Adolphe Alphand created this park in the 19th century, and it is renowned for its varied topography, which includes a lake, cliffs, bridges, and an artificial island home to a temple.

Features: There are many attractions at Parc des Buttes-Chaumont, such as a suspension bridge, waterfalls, grottoes, and verdant gardens. Perched atop the island, the Temple de la Sibylle offers sweeping views of the park.

Recreation and Relaxation: Teens can enjoy picnics, long walks, or just lounging on the grass. A peaceful diversion from the bustle of the city is offered by the park.

Temple de la Sibylle: A well-liked tourist destination, the temple sits atop the island. Reach the summit for awe-inspiring vistas of Paris and the surroundings of the park.

Grotto and Waterfalls: Visit the grotto next to the suspension bridge and take in the peaceful sounds of the cascading waterfalls. It's a quiet part of the park.

Suspension Bridge: Across the lake, the suspension bridge provides a distinctive and picturesque stroll. It offers beautiful views of the park's highlights and is a popular location for pictures.

Activities and Events:

Look for any events or activities occurring in the park, such as cultural programs or outdoor concerts. Events are frequently held in Parc des Buttes-Chaumont. Local Flavor: The surrounding districts have a genuine, local Parisian vibe. Spend some time looking around the park's surrounding streets for cafes, stores, and regional markets.

Accessibility: The park may be reached by bus and Metro (Buttes-Chaumont station, Line 7bis). To ensure a smooth visit, arrange your transportation in advance.

Free Admission: Park des Buttes-Chaumont is an inexpensive choice for a day of exploration and leisure because it is free to enter.

A beautiful experience in the center of Paris, Parc des Buttes-Chaumont offers a tranquil haven, a beautiful stroll, or a spot to relax.

Street art in Belleville

The 20th arrondissement of Paris's Belleville is well known for its thriving street art scene. When visiting Belleville's street art, teenagers should be prepared for the following:
Outdoor Gallery:

Belleville's vibrant murals, graffiti, and street art cover buildings, doors, and facades, like an outdoor art gallery. Here, the art scene is vibrant and ever-evolving.

Artists, both domestic and foreign:

Belleville's unique collection of artwork is enriched by the contributions of street painters from Paris and beyond. There will be a range of themes, styles, and approaches.

Rue Dénoyez:

Belleville's pedestrian Rue Dénoyez is a popular spot for street art. Graffiti and murals line the entire street, resulting in an imaginative and engaging atmosphere.

Opportunities for Exploration:

Teens can explore the area on a leisurely walk, finding hidden treasures around every turn. Since the art is not limited to any one place, investigation is essential.

Creative Murals:

Belleville is home to numerous murals that represent social, political, and cultural themes and send strong statements. Teens have the chance to interact with art that conveys a variety of viewpoints.

Social media and photography:

Photography is a common way for street art fans to shoot their favorite pieces. Urge teenagers to record their research and post it to social media with the relevant hashtags.

Creative Occasions:

Look for any festivals, art shows, or guided tours that Belleville may be hosting. These gatherings offer more perspectives on the neighborhood's street art scene.

Cafés and Gathering Places:

Teens may unwind and talk about the art they've seen in Belleville's quaint cafés and hangouts. They get the chance to fully experience the local culture.

esteem for artists and their work:

Teach teenagers to appreciate artists and their work. Even though street art is intended for public enjoyment, it is crucial to preserve and respect the existing pieces.

Regional Culture:

Belleville's street art provides a unique window into the local way of life and the character of the neighborhood. It's an opportunity to observe how art influences locals' day-to-day existence.

For teenagers who are interested in urban art and culture, Belleville's street art scene offers an engaging and dynamic visual experience.

Chapter 6

Culinary Delights

French cuisine overview

The world over, French food is recognized for its rich flavors, careful preparation, and variety of regional influences. The following is a summary of the main points of French food that teenagers may find intriguing:

Regional Diversity: There is a great deal of variation in French cuisine, with each region having its own specialties and cooking customs. There are many different sensations to discover, from the succulent sauces of Lyon to the mouthwatering seafood of Marseille.

French cuisine is known for its bread, and teenagers can indulge on a variety of baguettes, croissants, and pastries. "Boulangeries" and "pâtisseries," or French bakeries, are well-liked locations to indulge in delectable treats.

Cheese: With more than a thousand types, cheese from France is world-renowned. A variety of options are available for teens to try, including as the flavorful Roquefort and the creamy Brie, which are typically served with bread and a glass of wine.

French eating culture is heavily influenced by wine, as France is one of the world's top producers of wine. Teens understand the value of wine pairings with meals even though they won't be drinking it themselves.

Haute Cuisine: The lavish and meticulously prepared dishes that define French haute cuisine. It frequently calls for the employment of elaborate methods and premium, in-season ingredients. Bouillabaisse and coq au vin are two traditional examples.

Bistro Culture: Traditionally French comfort food is served in these laid-back, neighborhood bistros. Teens can unwind while consuming comfort food such as Ratatouille, Quiche Lorraine, and Croque-Monsieur.

Culinary Methods: French cooking methods, including baking, braising, and sautéing, have impacted cooks all over the world. The characteristic of French culinary expertise is the emphasis on exact preparation and presentation.

Desserts: Known for their sugary goodness, French desserts include Macarons, Tarte Tatin, and Crème Brûlée. Teens who have a sweet craving are welcome to delve into the fascinating world of French pastry.

Casual Street cuisine: French street cuisine offers delicious options in addition to formal dining. Popular options for a delicious and speedy snack include galettes, crepes, and pastries loaded with savory ingredients.

Culinary Education: Many teenagers may be familiar with the term "cordon bleu," which is linked with culinary brilliance. France is home to several prominent culinary schools. French culture has a particular place for the culinary arts.

Market Culture: The foundation of French cooking is seasonal, fresh products. Teens can take in the colorful market atmosphere where residents browse for a variety of fresh produce, meats, and fruits.

French cooking celebrates culinary creativity by putting an emphasis on top-notch, fresh ingredients and a love of food. Teens traveling across France can enjoy the diverse range of delicacies its culinary culture has to offer.

Teen-friendly cafes and restaurants.

There are several teen-friendly cafés and restaurants in Paris that provide a combination of delectable food, a laid-back vibe, and a pleasant setting. The following suggestions are provided:

Le Saint Régis: This traditional French café, which is situated on the Île Saint-Louis, has a warm ambiance and a menu that includes savory dishes, pastries, and crepes. There's a great view of the Seine River from the outdoor seating.

L'Ambroisie: This hip café, which is well-liked by both locals and visitors, is located in the Marais district. There are numerous salads, sandwiches, and cool drinks on the menu. The energetic atmosphere is enhanced by the active neighborhood.

Café de Flore: Known for its famous crimson awnings and literary past, Café de Flore is a classic café in the Saint-Germain-des-Prés neighborhood. Teens can have a light supper or snack at the same spot that was once frequented by well-known authors.

Le Comptoir du Relais: Serving a blend of French and international fare, this bustling cafe is located in the Saint-Germain-des-Prés area. It's a terrific place for teenagers to try French dining because of its laid-back yet elegant ambiance.

American breakfast: This entertaining diner-style restaurant in Paris is a great choice for teenagers who are hankering after burgers or American-style breakfast. It has several locations. It is renowned for its comfort food—classic American fare.

La Crêperie Josselin: Known for its mouthwatering sweet and savory crepes, this crêperie is situated in the Montparnasse neighborhood. It's appropriate for a leisurely dinner or snack because of the informal setting.

Le Relais de l'Entrecôte: This restaurant, which specializes in steak frites, offers a simple menu that makes ordering for teenagers easy. Both residents and tourists enjoy it for its delicious food and comfortable atmosphere.

Big Fernand: Well-known for its gourmet burgers, Big Fernand puts a contemporary and entertaining spin on classic burgers. Teens are able to personalize their burgers to fit their tastes.

L'Avenue: A stylish brasserie serving a blend of French and foreign cuisine, L'Avenue is located on Avenue Montaigne close to the Champs-Élysées. The chic environment and opportunities for people-watching enhance the whole experience.

Blend Hamburger Gourmet: Blend Hamburger Gourmet is a hip restaurant that serves high-quality, gourmet burgers to teenagers who love them.

Le Pain Quotidien: This restaurant, which has several locations throughout Paris, has a homey ambiance and a cuisine that includes fresh and organic foods. It's a nice place to have a light lunch or breakfast.

These eateries are perfect for teenagers seeking a blend of regional and global flavors because they offer a variety of selections to accommodate varying tastes and preferences.

Must-try French dishes and desserts

Tasting French food is a great way to experience a wide range of sensations. When visiting Paris, teens should definitely eat these must-try French cuisine and desserts:

Best French Recipes to Try:

Croissant: A buttery, flaky croissant is a classic French pastry that is great for breakfast or as a snack.

Fresh baguette from a neighborhood bakery is a great snack on its own or combined with cheese, ham, or other fillings to make a traditional sandwich.

Quiche Lorraine: Quiche Lorraine is a savory pie from the Lorraine region that has a creamy custard, bacon, and cheese in a delightful mix.

Coq au vin: Slow-cooked chicken served with red wine, onions, mushrooms, and bacon is a traditional French dish.

Marseille is the home of the delectable Bouillabaisse, a traditional Provençal fish stew made with a variety of fish, shellfish, and aromatic herbs.

Ratatouille: A delectable example of Provencal cuisine, ratatouille is a vegetable medley meal made with tomatoes, zucchini, eggplant, and bell peppers.

Duck Confit: To make duck confit, duck legs are slowly cooked in their own fat until they are tasty and soft. Its skin is frequently served crunchy.

Cassoulet: A hearty stew made with meat (such as pig, sausages, and occasionally duck) and white beans, cassoulet originated in the south of France.

Salade Niçoise: Originally from Nice, this light salad is usually made with tuna, olives, hard-boiled eggs, and different vegetables.

Escargot: Snails are served in their shells and prepared with butter, parsley, and garlic for the daring diner.

Best French Desserts to Try:

Crème Brûlée: Rich custard covered in a layer of caramelized sugar is the hallmark of this traditional French delicacy.

Macarons: Filled with a variety of flavored creams or ganache, macarons are delicate and colorful almond meringue cookies.

Éclair: An éclair is a long, thin pastry that is topped with chocolate-flavored frosting and filled with cream.

Tarte Tatin: A tasty and aesthetically pleasing delicacy, this tart is an upside-down caramelized apple tart.

Profiteroles are little balls of choux pastry that are filled with cream and frequently dipped in chocolate sauce. They are a delicious dessert.

Madeleines: A light and sugary snack, these little sponge cakes are usually fashioned like a shell.

French toast, or pain perdu, is a take on the traditional dish and is typically served with syrup, fruits, or powdered sugar.

Soufflé: A delicate and airy baked dish, soufflé can be savory or sweet (think chocolate or fruit flavors).

Tiramisu: Despite having Italian roots, French patisseries are known for their Tiramisu. It is composed of layers of mascarpone cream and ladyfingers dipped in coffee.

The dish known as Gateau Saint-Honoré, named for the patron saint of pastry cooks and bakers, has a puff pastry foundation topped with choux pastry and cream.

These meals and sweets provide a great sample of French cuisine, demonstrating the variety and skill of the nation's cuisine.

Chapter 7

Immersing in Culture

French cultural etiquette

A pleasant and courteous visit is contingent upon your comprehension and observance of French cultural etiquette. The following are important facets of French cultural etiquette:

Salutations and Courtesies:

Official Salutations:

Say "Bonjour" (good morning) or "Bonsoir" (good evening) to anybody you meet in public places like restaurants and stores. Adding "Monsieur" or "Madame" is seen as polite.

Cheek kisses and handshakes:

In professional situations, a quick handshake is customary when welcoming one another. Cheer kisses, or "faire la bise," are customary in social settings. Typically, the left cheek is kissed first.

Courtesy Headlines:

When addressing someone, especially in a professional or commercial setting, use titles like "Madame" or "Monsieur". These days, the term "mademoiselle" is used less often.

Dining Protocol:

Lunchtime On Time Arrival:

Be on time for meals and social gatherings. It is courteous to be on time for the host.

Table etiquette:

With your wrists resting on the edge, keep your hands on the table. You should not start eating until the host has finished.

Bread Etiquette: Instead of chopping bread with a knife, break it into smaller pieces. Instead of putting it on your plate, place it right on the table.

Wine etiquette: When served wine, it is traditional to hold off on sipping until the host raises their glass. Grab the stem of the glass.

French speech is typically more professional and reserved, with a soft spoken and courteous tone. Make liberal use of civil expressions such as "merci" (thank you) and "s'il vous plaît" (please).

Respect for Individual Space: Individual space is important to French people. Refrain from approaching people too closely, especially when conversing.

Smart Casual: A smart casual dress code is suitable in a lot of circumstances. Since Parisians typically wear elegant clothing, being well-groomed is frequently valued.

Language Protocols:

Use of Titles: When addressing someone, especially in a professional situation, start by utilizing their titles and last names. Upon invitation, you can switch to a first-name basis as you get to know each other better.

Learn the fundamentals of French:

Even though a lot of French people understand English, it is still appreciated if you can learn and utilize some simple French phrases.

Cultural Intelligence:

Sensitivity to Culture:

Be aware of cultural sensitivities when it comes to politics and religion in particular. French individuals typically would rather discuss these things in private.

Respect lines that form in public areas. It is considered rude to cut in line.

Tipping: Although service charges are included in restaurant bills, it is usual to round up the amount or leave little change as a gratuity. Rounding up is customary in cafes.

You may manage social encounters in France with grace and respect by adhering to these cultural etiquette guidelines, which will improve your entire experience.

Museums and art galleries for teen

Teens can enjoy a diverse range of cultural experiences in Paris, which is home to numerous museums and art galleries. The following galleries and museums target younger audiences:

1. The Louvre: Famous for its extensive collection, teens may especially adore famous pieces like Venus de Milo and the Mona Lisa. For a more interesting visit, the Louvre also provides interactive tours and multimedia guides.

2. Musée d'Orsay: Housed in a former railway station, this museum features a vast array of masterworks by Impressionists and Post-Impressionists. For teenagers who are interested in 19th-century art, the location and the artwork make it a stimulating visit.

3. Centre Pompidou-Musée National d'Art Moderne: The National Museum of Modern Art is housed in the Centre Pompidou, which is distinguished by its distinctive architecture. Teens can investigate modern and contemporary art, such as pieces by Kandinsky, Picasso, and Duchamp.

4. Musée de l'Orangerie: Housed in the Tuileries Gardens, this museum is well-known for Claude Monet's Water Lilies series. The panoramic murals in the oval rooms create an immersive experience.

5. The Rodin Museum: Situated in a lovely garden, this museum is devoted to the sculptures created by Auguste Rodin. Teens might be inspired by works of art such as "The Thinker" and "The Kiss."

6. The Picasso Museum: The Picasso Museum, which has a sizable collection of Pablo Picasso's artwork, is located in the Hotel Salé. Teens can investigate how the artist has changed throughout time.

7. The Musée Grévin: This interactive and amusing wax museum allows teenagers to view lifelike representations of famous historical and modern characters.

8. The Musée des Arts et Métiers: This historical museum of arts and crafts features innovations and technological developments. For teenagers who are interested in science and innovation, it's a stimulating place.

9. The Musée des Arts Forains: This collection of carnival and fairground items provides a one-of-a-kind experience. Interactive features and fascinating exhibitions are features of guided tours.

Teen-friendly events and festivals

All through the year, Paris is home to a number of teen-focused events and festivals that provide them with culture, entertainment, and unique experiences. The following festivals and events are suitable for teenagers:

1. Fête de la Musique (June 21): Honor the summer solstice with Paris's largest music event, which offers free performances all across the city. A wide variety of musical genres are appealing to teenagers.

2. Paris Jazz Festival (June–July): This event, which takes place outdoors in the lovely Parc Floral, offers jazz performances. Teens should take advantage of this wonderful chance to see live music in a laid-back environment.

3. Rock en Seine (August): Drawing both local and international bands, Rock en Seine is one of France's biggest rock music festivals. There are several stages, art pieces, and a vibrant atmosphere that teens may enjoy.

4. Paris Games Week (October): For those who love video games, this exhibition of the newest releases, tournaments, and virtual reality experiences is a must-see for teenagers.

5. October's Nuit Blanche: This night-long arts event turns the city into a stage for performances and installations of modern art. For teenagers, it's a singular and engaging experience.

6. Paris Manga & Sci-Fi Show (February and July): Manga, anime, and science fiction enthusiasts are catered to at this event. Teens can go around exhibits, interact with artists, and take part in cosplay.

7. Lollapalooza Paris (July): This international music event has a wide range of performers on its roster. Teens can take in the festival atmosphere, live music, and art exhibits.

8. Paris Photo (November): Showcasing artwork from galleries worldwide, Paris Photo is a premier international photography fair for teenagers with an interest in photography. It's a chance to learn about various photographic techniques.

9. Festival d'Automne à Paris: This multidisciplinary arts event takes place in Paris from September to December and includes visual, performing, and dancing arts. Teens have access to avant-garde and creative works.

Chapter 8

Staying Connected

Wi-Fi and mobile data options

In order to remain connected while in Paris, you have multiple alternatives for Wi-Fi and mobile data:

WiFi Configurations:

Free Wi-Fi in Public venues: Paris has a lot of public venues with free Wi-Fi, such as parks, libraries, and some areas used for public transportation. Search for networks with names such as "Free_WiFi" or "Paris_WiFi."

Cafés and Restaurants: Free Wi-Fi is available to patrons of a large number of cafés, eateries, and fast-food chains. You may stay connected while having dinner or a cup of coffee.

Hotels and Lodging: The majority of hotels, hostels, and holiday homes provide free Wi-Fi to their visitors. Verify the specifics of access and availability with your lodging provider.

Coworking Spaces: Take into consideration employing coworking spaces in Paris if you require a dedicated workspace. Some might provide alternatives for weekly or daily access.

Options for Mobile Data:

Local SIM Card: Get a local SIM card from a mobile phone company in France. You can now have a local phone number and data plan thanks to this. SIM cards are available at convenience stores, mobile shops, and airports.

Packages for Mobile Data: Several data packages appropriate for travelers are provided by French mobile providers. A specific quantity of data, text messages, and call minutes are frequently included in these bundles. For options, check with providers such as Orange, SFR, or Free Mobile.

Rent a Pocket Wi-Fi Device: Another name for a mobile hotspot is a pocket Wi-Fi device. These devices can be rented from a number of suppliers and offer multiple device Wi-Fi access.

International Roaming: Inquire about international roaming options with the mobile provider in your native country. Remember that roaming fees can be substantial, therefore it's critical to be aware of the associated expenses.

Global SIM Cards: A few businesses sell global SIM cards that are compatible with several nations, including France. This can be a practical choice if you're visiting several places.

E-SIM Cards: You can buy an eSIM plan online if your smartphone is compatible with eSIM technology. This eliminates the requirement for a physical SIM card when activating a local data plan.

Think about how much data you need, how long you plan to stay, and whether you require calling and texting in addition to data before selecting a mobile data plan. In addition, if you intend to use a local SIM card, make sure your handset is unlocked.

Emergency contacts

These are some crucial phone numbers to have on hand in case of emergency in Paris:

Emergency Medical/Ambulance Services:

For ambulance services and medical crises, dial 15 (SAMU, Service d'Aide Médicale Urgente).

Law enforcement / Police:

To get quick police assistance, dial 17.
Department of Fire:

In the event of a fire or other emergency, dial 18 to reach the fire department (pompiers).
Emergency Number in Europe:

For a generic emergency number that functions in all EU nations, including France, dial 112.
SOS - Every Service:

To contact law enforcement, emergency medical services, and firefighters, dial 112, which is a worldwide emergency number.
American Embassy in France:

To report an emergency involving U.S. citizens, please call +33 1 43 12 22 22 of the U.S. Embassy in Paris.
When requesting emergency assistance, always remember to maintain your composure and give precise details about the circumstances. It's a good idea to know where the closest hospital or medical center is if you're traveling abroad.

Chapter 9

Shopping and Souvenirs

Teen-friendly shopping districts

With numerous retail areas that suit a wide range of preferences and trends, Paris is a shopping haven. The following teen-friendly shopping areas provide a variety of fashionable boutiques, well-known brands, and distinctive stores:

1. Le Marais: This historic neighborhood is well-known for its winding lanes and is a popular destination for concept stores, stylish boutiques, and vintage retailers. Teens can discover independent, distinctive shops as well as well-known brands.

2. Champs-Élysées: This world-famous avenue is dotted with cafes, theaters, and retail establishments. Along this famous boulevard, teens may find landmark stores, stylish boutiques, and worldwide brands.

3. Galeries Lafayette: A posh department store featuring an eye-catching glass dome, Galeries Lafayette sells a blend of designer and modern clothing. Teens can take in the breathtaking architecture and discover the newest styles.

4. Saint-Germain-des-Prés: This neighborhood is renowned for its intellectual and creative vibe and is home to chic cafes, booksellers, and boutiques. Adolescents can find distinctive accessories and clothing.

5. Le Bon Marché: This posh department store in the Saint-Germain-des-Prés neighborhood provides a well chosen assortment of home, beauty, and fashion items. Teens who want to purchase for expensive goods should definitely check it out.

6. Les Halles and Forum des Halles: Situated next to the Centre Pompidou, Les Halles is a busy retail district featuring a mix of well-known brands and trendy businesses. The Forum des Halles retail center offers a variety of shopping options.

7. Rue de Rivoli: This pedestrian street, which runs along to the Louvre Museum, is dotted with a variety of stores, including eccentric boutiques and well-known labels. Teens can peruse a variety of stores offering accessories, apparel, and mementos.

8. Bastille: A variety of concept businesses, hip boutiques, and vintage shops can be found in this bustling district. Teens can take in the lively environment and find interesting fashion items.

9. Saint-Martin Canal:

Canal Saint-Martin is a cool and chic neighborhood with lots of independent boutiques, concept stores, and vintage shops. Teens can look at unique lifestyle and fashion goods.

Unique Parisian souvenirs

There are many distinctive mementos available in Paris that perfectly encapsulate the beauty and culture of the city. Consider the following unique mementos from Paris:

1. Macarons: A sweet and distinctly Parisian gift, macarons from renowned patisseries like Ladurée or Pierre Hermé are flavorful and vibrant.

2. Eiffel Tower Miniatures: Traditional mementos are miniature versions of the Eiffel Tower. They come in a range of shapes and sizes, from elaborate metal models to keychains.

3. French Fragrance: Invest in a bottle of perfume from well-known French labels such as Dior, Chanel, or Guerlain. It's a sophisticated and opulent present.

4. Parisian Art Prints: Look for prints or posters of famous artworks, street scenes, or Parisian landmarks by visiting Montmartre or other artistic neighborhoods.

5. French Cheese: Popular French cheeses are available in packages or vacuum-sealed forms, but raw cheese is not returnable. They make a distinctive present when combined with a cheese board.

6. Parisian Chocolate: Relish premium chocolates from acclaimed chocolatiers like Patrick Roger or La Maison du Chocolat. A delicious and portable treat is chocolate.

7. French Fashion Accessories: Take into account items from Parisian boutiques such as gloves, berets, and scarves. They can be both stylish and useful, and they exhibit French design.

8. Parisian Perfumed Soap: Beautifully packed and aromatic, French perfumed soaps are a delightful and opulent memento. Select traditional French fragrances or those with Provence inspiration.

9. French Wine or Champagne: Carefully pack a bottle of Champagne or French wine in your luggage and bring it home. Think about wines from particular areas, each distinguished by their individual characteristics.

Think about the hobbies and tastes of the receiver when choosing mementos, and search Paris's little markets and stores for a genuinely unique find.

Chapter 10

Respecting Local Laws

Overview of local laws and regulations

To guarantee a safe and pleasurable trip, it is imperative to be informed of and abide by local rules and regulations when visiting Paris. An outline of some important French legislation and regulations is provided below:

General Statutes:

Legal Drinking Age: In France, the legal age to purchase alcohol is eighteen. Buying alcohol for underage consumption is prohibited.

Smoking Ban: All enclosed public areas, such as cafes, restaurants, and public transit, are smoke-free zones. Certain areas are classified as smoking areas.

Drug Laws: It is strictly forbidden to consume, possess, or traffic in illegal narcotics. Doing so can result in harsh consequences.

Public Behavior: There may be fines or other consequences for acting in an unruly or disruptive manner in public areas.

Identity: You should always have some sort of identification with you, like a passport, in case law enforcement asks to see it.

Laws pertaining to transportation:

Seatbelts: All passengers in a car are required to buckle up.

France observes the right-of-way rule when driving. Pay attention to cyclists and pedestrians, obey traffic laws, and stick to the posted speed limits.

Public Transport Etiquette: Adhere to the guidelines and protocol when using public transport. Until you exit the station, hold onto your ticket.

Cultural Courtesies:

Salutations: The French customarily give each other a peck on the cheeks, or "faire la bise." By area, the quantity of kisses varies.

Tipping: Although service charges are sometimes included in restaurant bills, it is usual to round up the price or leave little change as a tip. Rounding up is customary in cafes.

Silent Times:

Pay attention to noise levels, particularly in the late afternoon and evening as these are normally peaceful times.

Safety Guidelines:

Emergency Numbers: To reach police, medical, and fire services in an emergency, dial 112, which is a worldwide emergency number.

Scams and Pickpocketing: Be on the lookout for pickpockets, particularly in populated locations and on public transit. Recognize typical con artists and safeguard assets.

Photography: Be mindful of people's privacy when shooting pictures, particularly in delicate places like places of worship. Don't take pictures of people without their permission.

COVID-19 Guidelines:

Health Procedures:

Comply with current regulations for health and safety, including the wearing of masks. Verify if there are any limitations or limits on travel because of the continuing COVID-19 outbreak.

Testing and Vaccinations: Find out if admittance into particular venues or events requires a certain test or immunization.

It's critical to keep up with any revisions or modifications to local rules and ordinances. Although these recommendations offer a broad outline, specifics may differ, therefore it's best to confirm the most recent information with reputable sources or local authorities.

Safety tips for teens

Teenagers must put their safety and wellbeing first when visiting Paris. The following safety advice is for teenagers traveling to the city:

1. Remain Informed: Keep yourself updated about local events and be mindful of your surroundings. Be aware of where key landmarks, emergency services, and your lodging are located.

2. Make Use of Reliable Transportation: Make use of trustworthy modes of transportation, such as authorized taxis, authorized public transportation, or ridesharing services. Refrain from taking rides from unknown people.

3. Buddy System: Go anywhere you can in a group or with a friend. The buddy system improves security and offers assistance in strange places.

4. Secure possessions: To avoid theft, keep your possessions secure. Pickpockets should be avoided, especially in crowded situations. Secure pockets, wear anti-theft bags, and exercise caution.

5. Emergency Contacts: Store vital contacts on your phone, such as your lodging information, the local emergency number, and the contact details of other travelers.

6. Respect and Obey Local Laws: Pay attention to and obey local laws and ordinances. This include observing quiet hours, driving safely, and paying attention to any posted signs.

7. Be Wary of Scams: Keep an eye out for typical scams and stay away from those begging for money on the street or from street sellers. If someone approaches, graciously say no and carry on your stroll.

8. Know Your Route: Make advance plans for your routes, particularly if you'll be taking public transit. To navigate with confidence, familiarize yourself with maps and landmarks.

9. Health and Safety: Put your health first by drinking plenty of water, getting appropriate rest, and paying attention to your physical condition. Know where the closest medical facilities are located.

Smartphone photography tips

Keeping a record of your experiences in Paris can be achieved by taking pictures with your smartphone at special occasions. For teenagers visiting the City of Light, consider the following smartphone photography advice:

1. Take a picture at golden hour:

The soft, warm light that comes from the golden hour, which occurs just after sunrise and before sunset, improves your pictures. Take advantage of this opportunity to get iconic locations, like the Eiffel Tower, glowing magically.

2. Try Out Some Angles:

Don't be scared to use unique angles in your work. To get a distinctive viewpoint, try taking pictures from low angles, and experiment with different framing strategies to create images that really pop.

Third, Apply the Rule of Thirds:

When arranging your photos, adhere to the rule of thirds. To create a balanced composition, divide your frame into a 3x3 grid and arrange important pieces along the gridlines or at their intersections.

4. Incorporate Humans for Scale:

A sense of scale and perspective can be conveyed by including individuals in your photos of enormous landmarks or buildings. This highlights the majesty of the architecture and gives your photos more intrigue.

5. Pay Attention to the Details:

Charming details abound in Paris. To capture the spirit of the city beyond the big attractions, pay attention to details like exquisite architecture, vibrant street signs, or distinctive textures.

6. People Shots in Portrait Mode:

For interesting portraits of people, use the portrait mode on your smartphone. With the aid of this tool, you may produce a lovely background blur that highlights your subject.

7. Try Your Hand at Night Photography:

Paris is especially beautiful at night. Try your hand at night photography by utilizing your phone's night mode or placing it steadily on a surface to take long-exposure pictures.

8. For landscapes, use the panorama mode:

Use the panorama mode on your smartphone to capture expansive vistas or panoramic views. The camera on your phone will automatically stitch the shots together as you slowly pan across the landscape.

9. Seize Genuine Moments:

Honest moments are among the best. Be prepared to record impromptu moments, such as people taking in the scenery from a street performance or a local enjoying a coffee.

Conclusion

As your voyage through Paris draws to an end, keep in mind that the purpose of the trip was to reveal the wonder of a city where art breathes life into the streets, history whispers through the cobblestone streets, and every corner tells a tale. It was much more than just visiting the City of Light. In addition to being your reliable travel companion through this fascinating city, "Paris Travel Guide for Teens" also aims to be the storyteller who weaves the tales of a bustling and dynamic metropolis, the spark that ignites your curiosity, and the guide that unearths hidden gems.

Not only can you find helpful tips for traveling around Paris in these pages, but you're also invited to enjoy the subtleties of French culture, accept the unexpected, and write your own story amidst the eternal beauty of this legendary city. When you bid farewell to the silhouette of the Eiffel Tower against a pastel sky, the scent of freshly baked croissants wafting from a quaint boulangerie, and the sound of your footsteps echoing along the Seine, never forget that the true magic is found in the memories you've made, not just in the places you've visited.

This book was meant to be more than simply words on paper; Paris has a way of making an enduring impression on its visitors. It was meant to be a gateway to experiences, a path to exploration, and a celebration of the spirit of adventure that characterizes the adolescent traveler. Thus, as you close this chapter, allow the tales of your time spent in Paris to reverberate like a gentle tune. May the lessons you've learned and the memories you've formed develop into priceless mementos of your incredible voyage through the heart of France. This guide aims to have been the compass that led you through the delights of a city that will always keep a piece of your heart. Paris has an enduring charm, so whether you decide to visit again or just carry its spirit with you, it will always be there. Goodbye, my lovely adventurer, till the next part of your journey begins.

Made in United States
Orlando, FL
22 December 2024

56416391R00037